Dinosaurs
Stars of the Show

Master Books®
A Division of New Leaf Publishing Group

Printed in China

For information write:

Master Books®
P.O. Box 726
Green Forest, AR 72638

Please visit our website for other great titles:
www.masterbooks.com

ISBN 13: 978-0-89051-546-4
ISBN 13: 978-1-61458-125-3 (digital)
Library of Congress Number: 2008935772

Master
Books®
A Division of New Leaf Publishing Group
www.masterbooks.com

Dinosaurs Stars of the Show

by Amie Zordel
Illustrated by Joanna Borrero

This book is dedicated to my Lord.
May His name be glorified.

And to my three wonderful daughters,
Cailin, Abby, and Elena, whose questions
about dinosaurs
inspired me to
write this book.

We would like to introduce you to the stars of our show.

The truth about dinosaurs, they help us to know.

One Saturday morning, I was watching TV.
My favorite show I was waiting to see.
I was all excited; it was about to begin.
I had my popcorn. I was going to dig in.

Dinosaurs were the stars of the show.
T-Rex, Triceratops and others we know.
Suddenly, a scientist appeared,
and said their age was "millions of years."

"Our planet Earth, animals and man,
evolved out of nothing, a part of no plan.
Side by side, man and dinos were not,"
the scientist said, as he went on and taught.

And I thought "*That's not right. That isn't true.*"
I stood right up! I knew just what to do.

I ran to my desk and opened the drawer.
The pages of my Bible I had to explore.

To find out when the world had begun,
I knew to turn to Genesis One.

In God's Word it is clearly stated.
"In the beginning God created . . ."

Day One

Day Two

Day Four

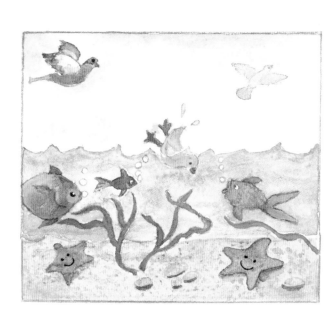

Day Five

Land animals were made on the sixth day.
From lions to lambs, there was quite a display.
Dinosaurs too were made on Day Six.
No parables, myths, gimmicks, or tricks.

14

Day Three

Day Six

So, Behemoth really was a living creature.
A beast of the earth with lots of features.

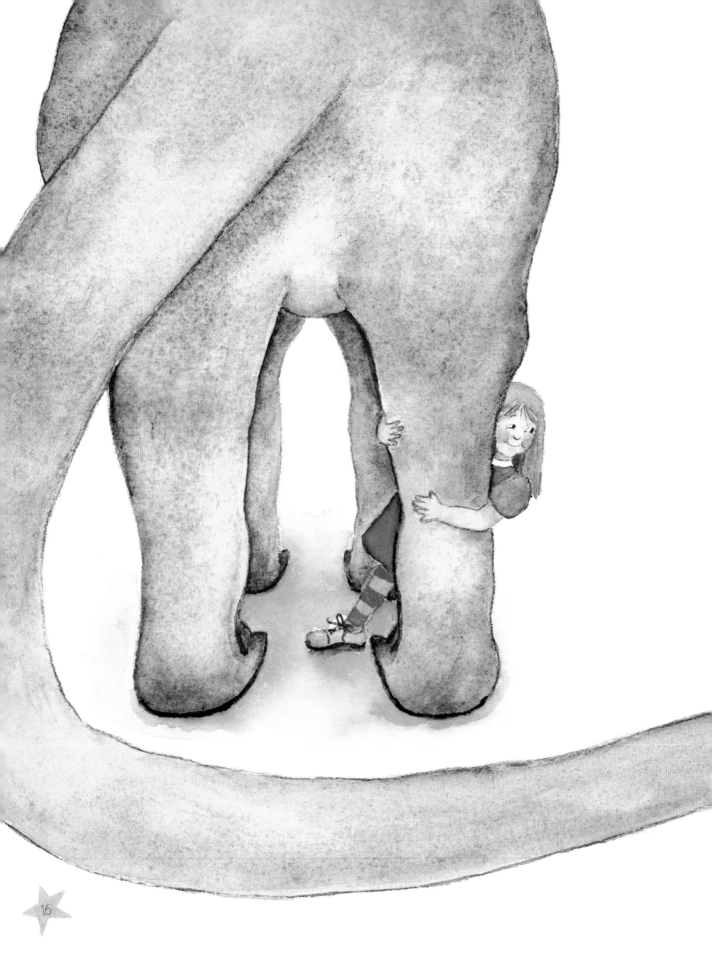

In Job 40:15, it's as plain as can be,
"Behold now behemoth, which I made with thee;"
Dinosaurs lived alongside of man.
Created together as part of God's plan.

As for the millions of years often quoted,
the Bible clearly has the truth noted.
The book of Luke, in Chapter Three,
lays it out for us to see.

Noah's Ark

Adam and Eve

If you count the generations you'll agree,
from Adam to Noah to Jesus to Me,
six thousand years is the actual span
between now and when the world began.

Tower of Babel

Jesus Christ

God's Word is clear, if we just try,
to search the Scriptures with an open eye.
All answers are there for you to find.
God gives wisdom as you use your mind.

So kids, if you have confusion,
about the dinosaurs and evolution,
read God's Word and you will see,
the truth is there for you and me.

GENESIS

The End . . .

Amie Zordel, author

of *Dinosaurs – Stars of the Show*, is a wife and mother of three beautiful young girls. She and her family reside in Northern Kentucky near the Answers in Genesis Creation Museum. Her 7-year-old daughter inspired her to write this book after being exposed to evolution while watching a kid's program. Through this book, Amie wants to enable parents to help strengthen their children's faith by providing Biblical answers to their questions.

The Zordel family

Joanna Borrero, illustrator of

Dinosaurs, Stars of the Show, has a degree in Art Education from Pratt Institute in Brooklyn, NY. As a popular book illustrator, this mother of three and grandmother of three agrees that her grandchildren are "the stars of my show." Joanna and her husband reside in upstate New York.